NATIVE AMERICANS

James Wilson

Thomson Learning
New York

Books in the series

Kalahari Bushmen
Kurds
Maori
Native Americans
Saami of Lapland
Tibetans

Published by Steck-Vaughn

Australian Aborigines
Bedouin
Inuit
Rainforest Amerindians

Series editor: Paul Mason
Designer: Kudos Editorial and Design Services
Consultants: Rachel Warner and Kaye Stearman,
    Minority Rights Group, and Frank Diamond

First published in the United States in 1994 by
Thomson Learning
115 Fifth Avenue
New York, NY 10003

First published in 1992 by
Wayland (Publishers) Ltd.

Library of Congress Cataloging-in-Publication Data
Wilson, James, 1949–
    Native Americans / James Wilson.
        p.   cm. — (Threatened cultures)
    Includes bibliographical references and index.
    ISBN 1-56847-150-5
    1. Indians of North America — Juvenile literature. 2. Indians
of North America — Social conditions — Juvenile literature.
3. Indians of North America — Government relations —
Juvenile literature. I. Title. II. Series.
E77.4.W55   1994
970.004'97 — dc20   93-36059

Printed in Italy

This book has been produced in consultation with the Minority Rights Group, an international nongovernmental organization working to secure justice for ethnic, linguistic, religious, and social minorities worldwide who are suffering discrimination.

Picture acknowledgments
The map on page 6 was drawn by Peter Bull. The publishers would also like to thank the following for permission to reproduce their photographs: Bryan and Cherry Alexander 20, 26, 41: Werner Forman Archive 18, 22; David Graham 5, 10, 12, 23, 42, 43; Hulton-Deutsch Collection 8, 34, 35; Impact 11, 14 (Sally Fear), 17 (John Cole), 25, 31 *bottom*, 44 (Sally Fear); Peter Newark's Western Americana 21, 22, 24, 36, 37, 38; Photri 4, 7, 13, 19, 27, 29 *both*, 30, 33, 45; Survival International 15 (Bob Bartel), 28 (uncredited), 39 *bottom* (Bob Bartel); James Wilson 9, 39 *top*, 40; Zefa 31 *top*.

Contents

1 *Introduction*

When Christopher Columbus "discovered the New World" in 1492, North America was already home to many millions of people. In the area now covered by the United States and Canada, there were more than six hundred different tribes or nations. They ranged from small bands of roaming hunters in the cold forests of the Canadian north to large farming communities near the great Mississippi River. Over thousands of years, these peoples had developed ways of life that were perfectly adapted to the area in which they lived, and they all felt a special closeness to the land and to the plants and animals with which they shared it.

For Native Americans, the Europeans' arrival was a disaster. Over the years millions of them died from European diseases such as chicken-pox and measles, against which they had no resistance. Millions more were massacred or driven from their homes by the new arrivals to North America. By 1890, the Native Americans had lost almost all their land and their population had fallen from an estimated six million or more in 1492 to about 350,000.

Native American or American Indian?

The first European explorers called the people they found already living in America Indios, or Indians (see Chapter 7). The name stuck and has been used for most of the last 500 years. Recently, some people have started to use the name Native American instead. They believe the word Indian is insulting and makes people think only of Hollywood Westerns (see Chapter 7), as well as being confusing (the people who live in India, after all, are called Indians).

Many Native Americans are used to being called Indian and use the word themselves. Some object to the new name, because they think that changing what they are called will not change attitudes and policies toward them. Most of them, in any case, think of themselves first as members of a particular tribe or nation (just as people in Europe think of themselves first as – for example – English, French, or Polish rather than European).

In this book, we use the term Native American to mean the first peoples of Canada and the United States. Wherever possible, we use the names of individual tribes or nations.

◄ *People in traditional-style costume at the Sioux Nation Powwow, an event where Sioux tribes come together to celebrate their identity as Native Americans.*

Today, there are about three million Native Americans in Canada and the United States. Although the Indian wars for the plains ended more than 100 years ago, they still face many serious problems: poor health, racism, threats to their remaining lands, and deliberate destruction of their traditional cultures. Their communities – known as reservations in the United States and reserves in Canada – are among the poorest in North America, with high unemployment and terrible social conditions. Because of these problems, more than half of all Native Americans now live away from the reserves and reservations, although most still think of their tribal communities as home and hope one day to return to them.

Although government policy has left many Native Americans poor and confused, it has not succeeded in destroying their cultures altogether. Some of them continue to live by hunting wild animals or by traditional farming. Many others still speak their own languages, keep their own religious beliefs, and retain their special relationship with the land. Today, they are determined to fight to preserve their remaining land and their rich and beautiful cultures.

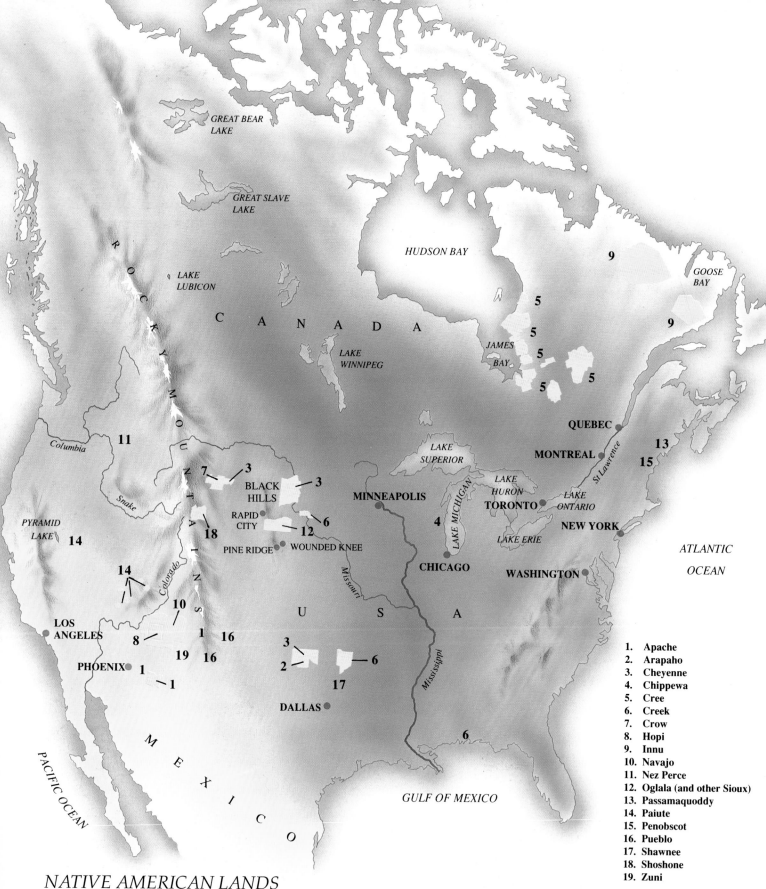

GREAT BEAR LAKE

GREAT SLAVE LAKE

HUDSON BAY

9

GOOSE BAY

9

5

5

5

5

5

JAMES BAY

C A N A D A

LAKE LUBICON

LAKE WINNIPEG

ROCKY MOUNTAINS

Columbia

Snake

11

PYRAMID LAKE

14

7   3

BLACK HILLS   3

RAPID CITY

18

PINE RIDGE

WOUNDED KNEE

6

12

MINNEAPOLIS

LAKE SUPERIOR

LAKE HURON

LAKE MICHIGAN

LAKE ONTARIO

LAKE ERIE

QUEBEC

MONTREAL

TORONTO

NEW YORK

St Lawrence

13

15

4

CHICAGO

WASHINGTON

ATLANTIC

OCEAN

14

Colorado

10

1   16

8

19   16

LOS ANGELES

PHOENIX   1

1

U   S   A

3

2

17

6

DALLAS

Missouri

Mississippi

6

M   E   X   I   C   O

PACIFIC OCEAN

GULF OF MEXICO

1. Apache
2. Arapaho
3. Cheyenne
4. Chippewa
5. Cree
6. Creek
7. Crow
8. Hopi
9. Innu
10. Navajo
11. Nez Perce
12. Oglala (and other Sioux)
13. Passamaquoddy
14. Paiute
15. Penobscot
16. Pueblo
17. Shawnee
18. Shoshone
19. Zuni

NATIVE AMERICAN LANDS

This map shows the lands of only the Native American groups mentioned in this book. There are many others: some, like the Oglala Sioux, live on reservations that the government acknowledges as theirs; other groups, like the Innu, are fighting to have their lands recognized.

The Sioux Nation

The Sioux (*say* 'Soo') are one of the largest and best-known Native American peoples. They are divided into three main groups: Dakota, Nakota, and Lakota. The Oglalas are one of the seven groups of the Lakota.

One Oglalas reservation is at Pine Ridge, in South Dakota (many United States cities and states were named after North American tribes). Pine Ridge is a wild, barren area of rolling grassland and tree-lined creeks in the windswept Great Plains region. It is bitterly cold in the winter, with temperatures falling as low as minus 20 ⁰F, and very hot in the summer. Part of the reservation lies in the Badlands, an almost uninhabited area where the high winds and extreme climate have worn the rocks into strange, eerie shapes.

HUNTERS OF THE PLAINS

About 150 years ago the Sioux lived by hunting the great herds of North American bison, or buffalo, that roamed the Plains. They moved from summer quarters to winter quarters, traveling on horseback, carrying their possessions behind them in a kind of sled called a travois, and setting up camp where they knew

▲ *Part of the Badlands, a wild, arid area on the Pine Ridge settlement. Many tribes were forced to settle on land that other people did not want.*

Traditionally, when the Sioux and other Plains peoples moved camp they carried their possessions on a kind of sled called a travois. The travois was made from bison skin, and the poles doubled as tepee poles.

game would be plentiful.

The Sioux depended on bison not only for meat, but for almost everything else they needed. Bison skins provided them with clothing, rugs, drums, and shields, as well as with the tents, or tipis, that they lived in. The sinews and bones of slaughtered animals were used to make tools and weapons. Bison skulls and horns were used for important religious ceremonies.

It was a hard, heroic life that called for great skill and courage. As well as having to hunt constantly for food, the Sioux were frequently at war, either with other tribes or – increasingly – with Europeans. Oglala men often fasted and prayed, asking the spirits to help them to be great warriors and hunters so that they could feed and protect their people.

It was also a life of great harmony with nature and beauty. The Native Americans felt they were related to everything around them: animals, plants, the earth itself. They celebrated this relationship in brilliant artwork and in ceremonies such as the magnificent Sun Dance.

This way of life ended in the second half of the nineteenth century, when the United States decided that the Sioux and the other Plains tribes must be removed and their land given to European settlers. The Sioux fought hard to defend themselves and defeated the U.S. Army several times. Finally, however, when bison herds were nearly exterminated by tourists and European hunters, the Sioux had to submit and settle on the Pine Ridge reservation, a tiny part of their original territory.

LIFE TODAY

Today, Pine Ridge is home to about 20,000 Oglalas. It is a very poor community. The tribe

The Sun Dance

One of the most important Native American religious ceremonies is the Sun Dance. Traditionally, this was practiced by many different tribes, particularly Plains peoples like the Sioux and the Cheyennes.

During the Sun Dance, people come together to give thanks to the Grandfather Spirit (known to the Sioux as *Wakan Tanka*, a power with no beginning or end) for the gift of life and for the food they have received. Dancers prepare by fasting and praying; sometimes they purify themselves by painful rituals.

Today, Sun Dances are still held on Pine Ridge and other reservations and more and more Native Americans are attending them.

no longer has enough land to live by hunting, and there are very few jobs. Most Oglalas are unemployed and have to try to survive on government welfare. There are serious problems of violence and of drug and alcohol abuse. Many young Oglalas commit suicide.

The Oglalas live in isolated homesteads or in small communities scattered across the reservation. Instead of the traditional tipis, they now mostly have small, single-story houses or mobile homes. There is a serious housing shortage and some families are homeless. Others have to live in old shacks, often without facilities like running water.

Recently, the government has tried to improve the situation by building modern housing developments at villages like Manderson and Wounded Knee. These new communities have amenities like electricity and running water, but they also have serious social problems. The houses are often cramped and too close together, a situation that increases tension among the people who live there.

The Wounded Knee Centenary Ride

In December 1890, more than 300 Lakota men, women, and children led by Chief Big Foot were massacred by the U.S. Army at Wounded Knee, on the Pine Ridge reservation. 100 years later, hundreds of Lakota riders retraced the last journey of Big Foot and his followers. For six days they rode in temperatures of minus 10 °F or lower, sleeping out under the stars at night. "We are releasing the spirits of the dead and wiping away our tears," said one rider. "We're also starting to rebuild our nation, so that we can deal with the problems of the present and the future together."

THE BUREAU OF INDIAN AFFAIRS (BIA)

Many of the Sioux' problems have been caused by the policies of the U.S. government. For most of this century, the United States has tried to destroy Native American cultures and force peoples like the Sioux to become just like other Americans. Instead of helping them to become

▲ *A community on the Pine Ridge reservation. Although many Oglalas now have modern houses, some still live in wooden huts or mobile homes without amenities like running water.*

▼ *Although bison were almost exterminated by hunters for their hides and tongues and by tourists for sport, there are now three herds on Pine Ridge.*

self-sufficient, it has encouraged them to sell or lease their land to American ranchers and to move to the cities to look for work.

The Sioux have not been able to resist or change these policies because the government is so powerful. The tribe elects its own council to run the reservation, but it cannot make any important decision without approval from the government's Bureau of Indian Affairs (BIA). The government also controls most of the few jobs on reservations, as well as paying welfare to the unemployed.

The government has used this great power to encourage Sioux who want to become more like other Americans and to discourage those who try to preserve their own culture. As a result, the community has often been bitterly divided.

TRADITIONS

In spite of pressure from the government, the Sioux have kept alive many aspects of their traditional culture. Families on the Pine Ridge reservation still breed horses, as their ancestors did 150 years ago. The children still ride from an early age and grow up to be expert horsemen and women. Today, this skill is often used in events like rodeos, where riders try to stay on an untamed horse for as long as possible.

Bison are also still very important to the Sioux. The Oglalas on Pine Ridge now have three herds, which are ranched like cattle. The meat is either eaten by the community or sold, and the skulls are used in traditional ceremonies.

In the early part of this century, Christian missionaries tried to stamp out Sioux religion, and ceremonies like the Sun Dance were outlawed. Spiritual leaders continued to practice their beliefs in secret, however, and today there is a great revival in traditional religion. Many

Sioux use the sweat lodge, a small steam-filled hut similar to a sauna, where they pray and purify themselves. Thousands also attend one or more of the Sun Dance ceremonies, which are held all over the reservation in the summertime.

Every August, thousands of people from Pine Ridge and other reservations come together for the Sioux Nation Powwow. Unlike the Sun Dance, this is a purely social occasion. For three days, dancers in brilliantly-colored headdresses and costumes perform to traditional singing and drumming, and people have a chance to meet their friends and relatives from different communities.

SIOUX OR AMERICAN?

Many young Sioux are confused about how they should think of themselves: as Sioux or as Americans. In some ways, their life is like that of other young Americans. They wear the same kind of clothes (except during ceremonies and powwows) and eat the same kind of food. They go to school every day and learn many of the same subjects, most of them taught in English.

When they get home, they watch American television.

At the same time, they grow up knowing they are different. At home, many of them are surrounded by older members of their family who speak the Lakota language and tell them stories of the time when the Americans and the Sioux were deadly enemies. Through ceremonies like the Sun Dance, they learn traditional spiritual beliefs that clash with the values of non-Native Americans. When they go to neighboring communities like Rapid City, they see how much wealthier most other Americans are. Often, they face racism from non-Native American people.

To overcome some of these problems, the Sioux are now trying to strengthen their own culture. The tribe has taken over the running of the schools on the reservation, and is trying to ensure that all Sioux children can speak their language and know something about their traditions. The tribe has also started its own radio station, KILI, which broadcasts both in Lakota and English and provides a mixture of American and traditional Lakota music.

◀ *Schools on reservations in the United States are now often run by the tribes themselves. Many of them teach children their traditional culture and language as well as subjects such as English and math that other American children learn.*

Who are Native Americans?

No one knows for sure where Native Americans came from or how long they have been in North America. Their closest relatives seem to be peoples like the Tibetans, which suggests that they originated somewhere in Asia. Most archaeologists think that their ancestors were Siberian hunters who crossed into Alaska during the last Ice Age, between 25,000 and 10,000 years ago. They were able to walk across from Asia into America because, during the Ice Age, there was not as much water covering the earth and the land between the two continents was above sea level. Then, when the ice melted at the end of the Ice Age, the level of the sea rose and covered this land bridge, cutting the Americas off from the rest of the world.

Many Native Americans do not believe this story. They say that, according to their own tradition, they have been in North America for much longer than 25,000 years. Archaeological finds that seem to date back to before the time of the land bridge suggest they may be right. Some experts think the Native Americans are right; they could have entered America as far back as 75,000 years ago, perhaps during a previous Ice Age.

THE NORTH AMERICAN CONTINENT

North America is a vast landmass, stretching from the arctic to the tropics. Today, most of it is covered by just two countries: Canada and the United States. Together, they have an area of almost seven million square miles, more than one-and-a-half times the size of Europe.

This huge region has an immense range of climate and geography: arctic tundra (an area where the subsoil is permanently frozen and there are no trees); dense pine forests; grassy plains; rich river valleys; wooded mountains; and scorching deserts.

As they slowly spread out across the continent, Native Americans began to adapt their way of life to these different conditions. Some of them remained hunters; others learned how to fish or became expert farmers, growing crops such as corn that are now eaten all over the world.

▼ *North America has a varied climate and geography: arctic mountains, forests, deserts, and plains. Native Americans once occupied every area of it, adapting their life-styles to suit the region in which they lived.*

By the time Europeans reached America in the 1490s, there were flourishing Native American communities all over the continent with widely differing life-styles and languages. (Some Native American languages were as different as English and Chinese.)

NATIVE AMERICANS TODAY

Today, as a result of European colonization (explained in Chapter 4) Native American societies have almost completely disappeared from some areas. Along the east and west coasts of the United States, for example, hundreds of tribes have been exterminated or reduced to tiny communities that have lost their language, their traditional way of life, and almost all their land.

Most of the surviving tribes live in the western and southwestern United States, in Alaska, and in Canada. Many of them are groups who used to live by hunting, like the Sioux. Today, they do not have enough land to hunt, so although they preserve much of their culture they no longer live in the same way.

In a few areas, however, Native Americans are still able to follow a way of life that is fairly traditional.

THE PUEBLOS

Among the most traditional groups are the Pueblo peoples, who live in the hot, dry desert region of the southwestern United States. The area has one of the harshest climates in North America,

▲ *The Pueblo tribes of New Mexico are among the most traditional Native American peoples. They have been living in villages of adobe (dried mud) houses like these since long before the time of Columbus.*

with low rainfall and temperatures sometimes reaching 115 °F or more in the summer.

If you drive through the Southwest today, you may still see a Pueblo: a community of flat-roofed adobe (*say* ah-doe'-bee) houses clustered together on top of a hill. (Adobe is a kind of clay that is made into bricks and dried in the sun.) Villages like these have been home for more than a thousand years to a number of different tribes, including the Hopi and the Zuni.

The Pueblo peoples are farmers, who have developed ingenious ways of growing corn, beans, squash, and other crops in the desert. Their life has always followed the cycle of the seasons, with spectacular festivals marking important times of year such as the start of spring. During these ceremonies, which sometimes last as long as nine days, the central square of each village fills with dancers in elaborate costumes. The most impressive are often the *kachinas*, who wear fantastic masks and represent messengers of the gods.

PEOPLES OF THE NORTH

Another area where Native Americans still follow a fairly traditional way of life is Northern Canada. This is a vast region of woods, rivers, and lakes, where the summer is too short and the winter is too cold for agriculture.

Before European contact, the peoples of this area – nations such as the Innu, the Cree, and the Dene – lived by hunting wildlife, particularly big game such as elk, moose, and caribou. Today, many of them still hunt; they also trap animals for the fur trade.

Traditionally, the northern peoples did not live permanently in one place. For much of the year, they would roam over a huge hunting territory, using their extraordinarily detailed knowledge of the land and the animals they followed to help them find food. In the summer, they would often camp by lakes or rivers to fish and to meet relatives and friends.

▲ *Innu children. When European traders first came to North America, they encouraged Native Americans, among them the Innu, to trap animals for their furs. Some northern groups still live partly by trapping. Today, however, their livelihood is threatened because many Europeans and Americans now think the fur trade is cruel.*

Since World War II, the Canadian government has been trying to force the northern peoples to settle in villages. These communities suffer from terrible problems, however, and many people prefer the old way of life. Some continue to take their families into "the bush," where they are able to support themselves by hunting and can pass on their culture to their children.

Traditional values and beliefs

As we have seen, the first peoples of North America had separate societies, with widely differing languages, cultures, and ways of life. Naturally, their values and beliefs also varied greatly from group to group and from area to area.

Traditionally, Native Americans did not use writing to record their knowledge and beliefs. Their cultures were passed on by myths and legends, handed down from one generation to the next. Through hearing these stories, Native American children learned who they were and how they should behave.

Every tribe has an origin legend, explaining how it came into existence. Some farming tribes, for example, believe they first emerged on the surface of the Earth from a dark Underworld. Others believe they came from the sky.

> **Tewa origin legend**
>
> Every tribe has a story about how it began. This one is told by the Tewa people of the Pueblos:
>
> *At the beginning, our ancestors came up out of the Earth, until they were living under a lake. The world under the lake was like this one, but dark. Spirits, people, and animals all lived together, and there was no death.*
>
> *Among the spirits were the two mothers of the Tewa, Blue Corn Woman and White Corn Maiden. They asked one of the men to go and find a way for the people to leave the lake.*
>
> *After many adventures, he returned. The people rejoiced. They left the lake, and came out onto the surface of the Earth. They set out on a long journey, stopping at twelve places along the way, and finally reached the land where they still live to this day.*

> **Allotment**
>
> At the end of the Plains Wars in the nineteenth century, the United States government decided that Native Americans must start to live like other American citizens.
>
> Under the Dawes Act of 1887, tribes were forced to divide their reservations into individual plots. Each family was to be given a plot and was encouraged to become farmers. Any surplus land would then be sold off.
>
> Many tribes did not believe that land could be individually owned. They tried hard to prevent their reservations from being divided up, but the government ignored their protests. Sometimes the U.S. Army was called in to force a tribe to accept allotment.
>
> As a result of allotment, Native American lands were reduced from about 138 million acres in 1886 to less than 52 million acres in 1934.

Despite such differences, however, most traditional Native Americans do share some basic ideas about the world and how we should live in it.

THE EARTH

Unlike Europeans, most traditional Native Americans do not see the Earth as separate from themselves, something cold and dead that they can simply exploit for their own use, but rather as a living being of which they are a part. Many of them speak of it as their Mother, because from its own flesh it gives life to them and to everything that lives.

Before they were forced to settle on reserves and reservations, most Native Americans did not see the land as something that could be divided up and owned by individuals. As the

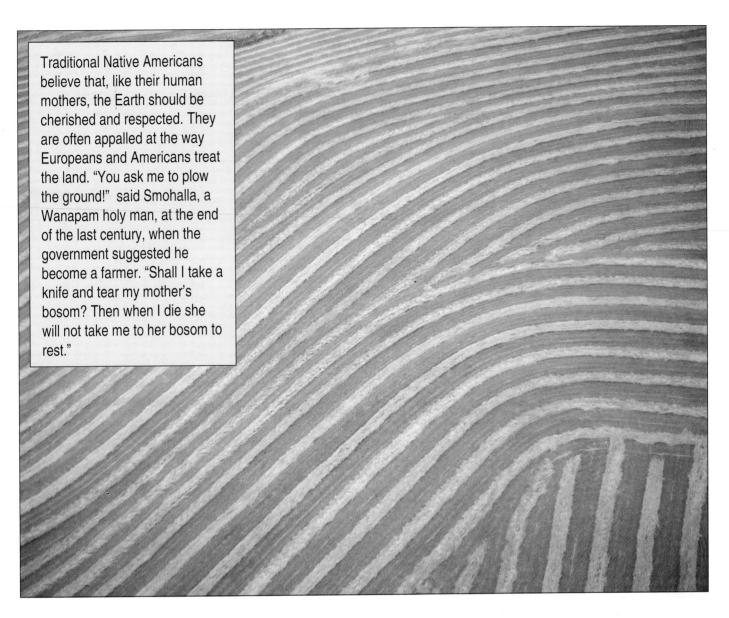

Traditional Native Americans believe that, like their human mothers, the Earth should be cherished and respected. They are often appalled at the way Europeans and Americans treat the land. "You ask me to plow the ground!" said Smohalla, a Wanapam holy man, at the end of the last century, when the government suggested he become a farmer. "Shall I take a knife and tear my mother's bosom? Then when I die she will not take me to her bosom to rest."

modern Oglala spiritual leader Birgil Kills Straight puts it: "The Earth does not belong to us. We belong to her."

ANIMALS, PLANTS, AND BIRDS

For almost all traditional Native Americans, animals, plants, and birds are also children of the Earth and therefore their relatives. Like the Earth herself, they are not there simply to be used, but must be treated with respect. For example, when traditional Pueblo people remove a fir branch for one of their rituals, they are careful to pray to the Creator, explaining that their intention is not to damage the tree but to use it for a sacred purpose.

Traditional Native Americans even see the animals they hunt as members of the same family. In some tribes, hunters say a prayer to a game animal before killing it, such as: "Forgive me, my brother, but my people must eat." They believe that when they die, their bodies will return what they have killed and eaten to the Earth, so that new generations of people, plants, and animals can live.

SPIRITS, SHAMANISM, AND WITCHCRAFT

Most traditional Native Americans believe that, beyond the physical world of rocks, trees, and animals, there is a world of spirits. The Earth

Vision Quests

Traditionally, in many tribes, children in their early teens would go on vision quests. Each would go alone to an isolated place where he or she fasted and prayed, sometimes for several days and nights. At the end of that time, the teen may see a vision, often of an animal or bird, that would give spiritual power and reveal how the seeker was to live as an adult.

For the rest of their lives, people who had been on a quest would have a special relationship with the animals or birds they had seen in their vision. A boy who had seen a wolf, for example, would call on the power of the wolf to help him in hunting, in battle, or in times of need.

Although vision questing has almost died out in many areas, there are a few traditional communities where it is still practiced today.

This picture shows Chief Mountain, in Northern Montana, which is visited by members of the Blackfoot tribe who meditate and pray for guidance there.

herself has a spirit, and so do all the creatures that live on her. It is this spiritual world that binds together the whole of creation.

Native Americans believe it is very important for all the different spirits to be kept in harmony with each other. They think human beings can help to preserve this harmony by living according to the rules that were given to them by the Creator. Usually, this means they must pray and observe certain rituals, show respect to all living things, and try to be good members of their tribe or nation. Most believe it is especially important to be brave, modest, and generous: being boastful or aggressive in one's own community or not sharing food with other people is considered particularly bad behavior. Anyone failing to live

◀ *Henry Crow Dog, a Lakota shaman. The shaman is important in all traditional Native American communities. His powers enable him to communicate with the spirit world and to cure people who are sick.*

up to these rules upsets the balance of the spirit world. When this happens, problems such as hunger, drought, and disease are created.

In most communities, there is someone – usually a man – called a shaman, who has special powers and can help to restore spiritual harmony. Singing and beating a drum, he travels to the spirit world to discover why, for example, someone is sick or there is a shortage of food. Through rituals, ceremonies, and – in the case of sickness – traditional medicine, he tries to cure the problem by bringing the spirits back into balance. Among some groups, such as the Navajo and the Apache, these ceremonies can last up to twelve days and nights.

In the past, a shaman could be feared as well as respected. Many people were frightened of witchcraft, and believed that a bad shaman could use his powers to put spells on people as well as to cure them.

The invasion of North America

Europeans did not realize that America existed until Christopher Columbus' ship landed in the Caribbean in 1492. Shortly afterward, European traders and explorers began to arrive.

TRADERS

The first traders bartered with the east coast tribes, exchanging iron tools and weapons from Europe for beaver skins to be made into hats.

The east coast peoples quickly became dependent on European implements, which were more efficient than their own stone tools. The old balance between tribes was destroyed as they started to compete with one another for more guns and tools and for control of the fur trade. As the European traders moved farther and farther west, more and more tribes were affected.

DISEASE

An even bigger problem for Native Americans was disease. After thousands of years of being separated from the rest of the world, they had almost no natural resistance to European illnesses like measles, smallpox, and the common cold. Without – to begin with – realizing it, traders and explorers started terrible epidemics that spread from tribe to tribe. Sometimes as much as 90 percent of a community would die in a single outbreak.

SETTLERS

By the time large numbers of settlers started to arrive in the seventeenth century, European illnesses had already killed hundreds of thousands of Native Americans on the east coast. As a result, there were large areas of

◀ *A Cree woman in Canada prepares a caribou hide to be cut up and made into snowshoes. Some peoples in northern Canada and Alaska still follow a traditional hunting way of life, although economic development is making it more difficult for them. Traditional hunters use not only the meat but every part of the animals they kill.*

uninhabited land where the Europeans could settle.

Many of the surviving Native Americans were too shocked and confused to defend themselves against the Europeans. In some cases, they gave land and food to the settlers because their own population had been almost wiped out and they thought the newcomers would help them. They did not realize that in a few years there would be even fewer Native Americans and more settlers wanting their land.

The difference between Native American and European attitudes toward land caused a lot of conflicts and misunderstandings. Many English settlers thought they could have any land where there were no houses or fields. As a result, they often took areas that the Native Americans used for hunting or food-gathering.

Another problem was that many Native Americans thought they could continue to use an area even after they had allowed Europeans to settle in it. They did not think land could be individually owned, and were surprised and angry when settlers put up fences and told them they must keep out. Sometimes these misunderstandings led to fighting, which often ended with the Native Americans being massacred.

Allies and Enemies

For almost three centuries after the arrival of Europeans in America, the British, French, and Spanish fought for control of the continent. Much of the actual fighting was done by Native Americans, who were bribed and threatened into helping one or another of the European powers. European generals encouraged the tribes to exterminate each other so that the lives of their own soldiers would be saved and more land would be opened up for settlers. Whichever side won, Native Americans were always the losers. The victors often betrayed their own allies, and always punished their enemies. On at least one occasion, for example, blankets infected with smallpox were deliberately sent to a defeated enemy tribe to wipe it out.

▲ *Many Native American tribes, including the Sioux, only began bison-hunting as a major way of life on the plains when they were pushed west by the increasing numbers of Europeans arriving in the east.*

John Collier

When Franklin Delano Roosevelt was elected President of the United States in 1933, he appointed John Collier Commissioner of Indian Affairs. Although he has since been criticized for failing to understand some Native American traditions, Collier was genuinely interested in trying to help Native Americans.

Collier instituted what was known as the Indian New Deal. Among its measures where the ending of allotment; the right to buy back land that had been lost during allotment; the Indian Reorganization Act, which allowed people living on reservations limited self-government; and loans to Native American businesses.

MISSIONARIES

As well as trading and settling in North America, Europeans sent missionaries to convert people to Christianity. Many missionaries thought the Native Americans were savages who worshiped devils and would be not go to heaven if they did not become Christians.

In general, Native Americans respected other peoples' religions. In the beginning, many tribes welcomed the missionaries, seeing them as holy people with spiritual power like their own shamans. It quickly became clear, though, that most of the missionaries expected them to abandon their own beliefs and way of life completely and to live like Europeans.

The work of the missionaries caused bitter divisions in many tribes. Some refused to be converted and insisted on keeping to their old ways. Others accepted the new religion, thinking it might give them protection against the new diseases that their own shamans and ceremonies seemed powerless to cure.

THE FRONTIER

As the European "frontier" moved farther into North America, tribes were either destroyed or driven west.

Among the groups that moved were the Lakota, who were pushed out of their homeland in Minnesota in the seventeenth and eighteenth centuries by other tribes farther east. At about the same time, they acquired guns and horses from European traders. It was this change that allowed them to move on to the plains to begin their bison-hunting way of life.

After the United States became independent in 1783, millions of new immigrants flooded into North America from Europe. As these people pushed west, the government took or bought more and more Native American land for them to live on. Often, the tribes were tricked or forced to make treaties in which they gave up some of their territory in exchange for promises of help and protection. They thought these agreements would last forever, but almost always, after a few years, the government decided more land was needed and broke its word. The tribes would then be tricked into signing a new treaty giving away even more of

Battles and Massacres

In 1866, Captain William Fetterman boasted that he could ride through the Sioux Nation with only 80 men. He was lured into a trap by a group of Sioux, Arapaho, and Cheyenne led by Crazy Horse. American historians call the incident the Fetterman Massacre.

Almost exactly 24 years later, the U.S. Cavalry killed more than 300 unarmed Sioux men, women, and children at Wounded Knee. In most history books, this is described as a battle. As one Native American said: "When whites kill Indians, it's a battle. When Indians kill whites, it's a massacre."

Recently, some historians have tried to give a more balanced picture, but many Native Americans still feel they are unfairly depicted.

▲ *This picture shows the memorial to Native Americans who died at Wounded Knee in 1890.*

their territory. Government agents would make false promises to Native Americans to persuade them to sign, and if that did not work they would sometimes forge the signatures themselves.

THE WAR FOR THE WEST

In 1848, gold was discovered in California. Immediately, thousands of fortune-hunters poured into the area. As they went, they killed Native Americans for sport and massacred whole villages. The Native American population of California declined by more than 80 percent in thirty years.

The trails to the West coast crossed the Great Plains. The endless wagon trains of settlers disturbed the great herds of bison, and soon the Sioux and the other Plains tribes were forced to start fighting for their land and their way of life.

Although they were heavily outnumbered, the Plains tribes fought with great skill and courage. At one point they even forced the government to sign a peace treaty and withdraw from their territory. When hunters and soldiers began to destroy the bison, the U.S. government did nothing to stop the slaughter. Between 1850 and 1910, the bison population fell from sixty million to just a few hundred.

Finally, the Plains tribes and the other free Native American nations were forced to settle on small reservations where they were held almost as prisoners of war. The last "battle" in the War for the West took place in 1890, when around 300 Sioux men, women, and children were massacred at Wounded Knee on the Pine Ridge reservation.

Red Cloud, who led the Lakota in the Land Wars of the 1860s and forced the U.S. Army to close their forts in Lakota territory. When gold was discovered in the Black Hills the government broke the treaty the Sioux had won. "They made us many promises, more promises than I can remember," said Red Cloud, "but they never kept but one: they promised to take our land, and they took it." ▶

Threats to Native American lands and resources

6

Today, Native Americans retain only a tiny proportion of North America. Reserves and reservations make up less than three percent of the total area of Canada and the United States. In addition, there are a few remote parts of northern Canada where Native Americans do not live on reserves and continue to hunt and trap in their traditional territory.

In general, Native American communities are in isolated areas or on poor land that settlers did not want. However, as the demand for resources grows, even these lands are increasingly threatened by various kinds of development.

WATER WARS

The biggest problem facing many Native Americans is shortage of water. Some of the largest tribes, including the Pueblos, the Apaches, and the Navajos (the biggest tribe of all, with a reservation of about 12,000 square miles), live in the desert Southwest. As more and more people have moved into the area, Native Americans have had to share the very limited supplies of water with farmers and with growing cities like Phoenix and Tempe.

In some cases, non-Native Americans have diverted rivers away from the reservations and toward their own communities. As a result, the plants and wildlife upon which the tribes depend have started to die. At Pyramid Lake in Nevada, for example, a community of Paiutes who traditionally lived by fishing have seen the level of their lake fall by more than 100 feet since the beginning of this century. One species of fish in the lake is extinct, and the cui-ui, a fish found

◄ *People from Taos Pueblo in New Mexico working to maintain a river bank. For a thousand years or more the Pueblos have survived by skillfully using a limited water supply. Now their way of life is threatened as non-Native Americans take more and more water for their cities and companies.*

nowhere else in the world, is now seriously endangered.

The shortage of water affects other areas as well. For instance, it is a serious problem in the Plains, where tribes including the Oglala and other Lakota tribes live. Without adequate water, it is almost impossible for tribes to develop activities like farming and forestry to support themselves. Some Native Americans fear that, as the problem gets worse, their land will be reduced to a desert where no one can live.

DAMS

For some Native Americans, especially in Northern Canada, water creates a different kind of problem. With the support of the government, energy companies are damming rivers and flooding huge areas of traditional hunting territory to generate hydroelectric power for people living thousands of miles away.

One example, affecting thousands of Native Americans, is the James Bay project in northern Quebec. The Cree and Inuit people of the area, like other northern groups, have always lived by hunting, fishing, and trapping. This way of life became more difficult in 1975 when part of their land was flooded. Not only did they lose valuable hunting territory, but rotting vegetation in the flooded area poisoned the fish in their rivers and lakes.

A new project, if it is built, will take most of the rest of the Cree's land. Many Cree believe they could not survive this disaster. As Grand Chief Matthew Coon Come said in 1992: "The destruction of our hunting land through the destruction of all the rivers in Northwestern Quebec would put an end to the hunting and fishing way of life of my people. It would put an

▲   *The James Bay hydroelectric project in Northern Quebec has flooded thousands of square miles of hunting territory used by the Cree people. Now the Cree are threatened by "James Bay II," which would flood most of their land and destroy their way of life forever.*

The Black Mesa Mine

One important development is at Black Mesa in Arizona, where the Peabody Coal Company has created the largest strip mine in the world on land belonging to the Hopi and Navajo tribes. (A strip mine is where coal is excavated by removing the surface of the land rather than digging a deep underground pit.)

Thousands of traditional Hopis and Navajos opposed the mine. As six Hopi elders explained: *Hopi land is held in trust in a spiritual way for the Great Spirit, Massau'u.... The area we call* Tukunavi *[which includes Black Mesa] is part of the heart of our Mother Earth.... The land is sacred and if the land is abused, the sacredness of Hopi life will disappear and all other life as well.*

Despite these warnings, the BIA allowed the mine to be developed. The mine, which has been called an environmental disaster, is devastating for the Hopi and Navajo tribes. It not only causes pollution, but also destroys plants and uses millions of gallons of water.

▲ *A Navajo man. Several tribes, including the Navajo, are affected by mining projects on or near their land. Mining causes pollution and health problems, and many traditional Native Americans object to it because it damages the Earth.*

end to the spiritual connection which my People have had with their land for at least the past 5,000 years."

MINING

Mining affects many Native American communities in North America. Some areas, which seemed almost worthless when they were recognized as reservations at the end of the nineteenth century, were later found to contain rich deposits of oil, coal, or minerals such as uranium ore.

The tribal councils of some tribes, such as the Navajos in Arizona and New Mexico, have allowed companies to mine and drill on their land. This kind of development is often opposed by the more traditional members of the community, who feel it is destructive to the Earth and threatens their way of life.

In some cases, tribal councils have voted to accept mining only because of enormous pressure from the Bureau of Indian Affairs or because they have not been told how much damage it will cause. The BIA is meant to protect Native Americans, but it has sometimes advised tribes to sell their resources for far less than their real value. It has also failed to keep companies that ignore many of the regulations designed to protect the environment from mining on Native American land. This has led to dangerous pollution and caused serious health problems among the Navajo and other groups, where there are high rates of cancer and lung disease.

Mining also uses up millions of gallons of water every year. In the Southwest, underground aquifers (reserves of water) that have existed for millions of years are swiftly becoming depleted.

Despite all these problems, the mining companies want to extend their operations. Recently, about 10,000 Navajo people have been forcibly removed from land where Peabody Coal hopes to mine.

▲ *Innu people in Northern Canada protesting the use of their land for military activities. They are waving an Innu flag.*

LOGGING AND OIL

Some groups, particularly peoples like the Haida and the Cree in northern and western Canada, are being seriously affected by oil and logging companies that are invading their territory. These operations, often on tribal lands that have never been sold or surrendered to the government, destroy the tribes' traditional way of life by removing huge areas of forest and driving away the game animals on which people have always depended.

The Lubicon Lake Cree

The Lubicon Lake Cree in Alberta, Canada, have been devastated by oil drilling and commercial logging. They have never signed a treaty surrendering their land to the Canadian government, and until 1979 most of them lived traditionally by hunting and trapping.

Then oil companies started to explore in Lubicon territory, and by 1982 more than 400 oil wells had been drilled within 15 miles of the main settlement. Shortly afterward, the Alberta government leased a large area of traditional Lubicon land to the logging company Daishowa.

The logging and oil companies have driven away the game animals. Today over 90 percent of the Lubicon Lake Cree are dependent on government welfare (compared with 10 percent in 1979), and they face terrible social problems.

MILITARY ACTIVITIES

Because Native Americans have little political power and their lands are often isolated and sparsely populated, the United States and Canadian governments sometimes use these lands for dangerous military activities.

In the United States, one of the worst-affected groups are the Western Shoshone of Nevada. After World War II, the government took a large part of their traditional territory to build a nuclear weapons testing site. Since then, hundreds of nuclear weapons have been tested. There has been appalling pollution, and the tribe's herding and food-gathering way of life has been devastated.

In Canada, the Innu people of Labrador and Quebec are threatened by the use of their traditional hunting territory by the military for a training ground for pilots. Jets from several NATO air forces fly at supersonic speeds only a few feet above the ground, terrifying everyone and seriously disrupting the lives of the wildlife the Innu hunt.

LAND RIGHTS

Many Native American peoples are still struggling for their land. In the United States, tribes such as the Sioux and the Western Shoshone are fighting to regain millions of acres of territory that the government took from

In a few short years we have been completely robbed of our land and our freedom. We have seen control of our country, the land that gave us birth as a people thousands of years ago, taken from us. And now we are treated as invisible, as if we do not exist. We are a hunting people. To keep us in one place, in a village, has meant that they have tried to separate us from everything that gives our life as a people meaning, and it has also meant that we have been changed in only a few years from one of the most self-reliant and independent peoples in the world to one of the most dependent.   Rose Gregoire, Innu.

◄ *Native American leader Russell Means, wearing a feather earring, on the Trail of Broken Treaties in 1972. This was a march to draw attention to all the treaties with Native Americans that the U.S. government had signed and then broken.*

them illegally.

In Canada, the government is trying to force several groups, such as the Innu of Labrador and Quebec, to give up most of their traditional land. The government says it will recognize the peoples' right to their land only if they will agree to sell it and accept small reserves where they will no longer be able to practice their traditional way of life. Because they are forced to settle and the children are sent to school, these peoples increasingly suffer from the problems of violence, suicide, and drug and alcohol abuse that affect other oppressed groups.

HUNTING AND FISHING RIGHTS

Some tribes are threatened by attempts to limit their right to hunt and fish in traditional areas. This is a particularly serious problem in areas like Alaska, northern Canada, the Pacific Northwest, and the Great Lakes, where many communities still depend on hunting and fishing for much of their food.

In many places, hunting and fishing rights are guaranteed by treaties made with the government at the end of the last century. However, many Americans and Canadians believe it is wrong for Native Americans to continue to have special rights today. Many of these opponents are people who – unlike the Native Americans – hunt and fish for sport rather than for food. In some communities, Native Americans have been arrested for hunting and fishing in traditional areas. There have also been many cases of violence, affecting, for example, members of the Chippewa tribe in Wisconsin.

▲ *Traditional fishing on the coast of the Pacific Northwest. In many parts of North America Native American hunting and fishing rights are threatened by sports hunters and commercial fishing companies.*

Cultural threats

Native Americans also face many cultural threats to their survival.

Perhaps the biggest threat comes simply from where they live. The United States and Canada are among the richest and most powerful societies on earth. Inevitably, their attitudes and their way of life powerfully affect Native American communities, whose traditional values are often very different.

For example, many Americans and Canadians think that to be successful you should work hard and make as much money as possible for yourself and your family. They believe that the richer you become, and the more you spend on such

▲ *The values and wealth of some non-Native American societies contrast dramatically with those of some traditonal communities.*

possessions as large houses and expensive cars, the more other people will respect you.

Most traditional Native Americans see this as quite wrong. They have been taught that you should not try to accumulate more than anyone else, but should share everything you have with the rest of your community. As George Manuel, a member of the Shuswap tribe from western Canada, put it: "In our culture, the more you give away, the richer you are."

The conflict between these two views is a problem for many Native Americans. They want to preserve their own values, but the society around them puts them under huge pressure to become more "American" or "Canadian."

RACISM

In some areas, particularly those such as the Southwest and the Plains where Native Americans live in large numbers, they suffer serious racism from other people. Non-Native Americans often have very little understanding of their culture and describe them as lazy, drunken, or dirty. This racism sometimes leads to violence, and occasionally even to murder. In 1972, for example, a Lakota named Raymond Yellow Thunder was stripped naked, forced to dance in front of a group of drunken U.S. army veterans, and then killed.

Racism not only hurts and angers many Native Americans, it also often reduces their belief in themselves. Inevitably, some of them start to feel that there must be something wrong with their own culture and that they will be accepted by other Americans only if they abandon it.

EDUCATION

The United States and Canadian governments have always used education as a way to weaken and destroy Native American culture. From the 1880s until the 1960s, children were taken from their homes and sent to strict, military-style boarding schools to be turned into "Americans" or "Canadians." They were brutally punished for speaking their own languages and taught to despise their own people.

The boarding school system devastated Native American communities. Families were broken up, and thousands of children died from disease, brutality, and despair. If they tried to run away, the children were hunted and rounded up like escaped animals.

Many languages and cultures were almost

▲ *A boarding school for Native American children in 1915. Children were taken from their families to attend such schools, where many of them died.*

The Nixon years

Although it later became famous as being a time of government corruption and dishonesty, the presidency of Richard Nixon saw important legislation for Native Americans. Among the most significant were measures that allowed them to set up their own schools. These now teach Native American children about their own cultures and traditional beliefs, as well as other subjects that all American children learn.

▲ *A Jicarilla Apache girl in class at a Catholic school in Albuquerque.*

destroyed. Because the children were away from home, their parents and grandparents were unable to pass on to them their traditional stories and beliefs. When they finally returned to their reserves and reservations, many children spoke only English and could no longer communicate with their own families. Not surprisingly, many of them ended up unsure about who they were and where they belonged.

Today, most boarding schools have gone, but children are still often confused about their identity. Most of their classes are in English and they take the same classes as other American children. Every morning, in many schools, students pledge allegiance to the American flag. Students are taught to respect national leaders such as Andrew Jackson, who was President of the United States from 1828-1837.

He hated Native Americans and tried to destroy them.

MISSIONARIES

For most of this century, Christian missionaries were one of the biggest threats to Native American culture. The Canadian and United States governments gave the missionaries enormous power over the reserves and reservations, including the right to run some of the boarding schools. Traditional ceremonies such as the Sun Dance and the Potlatch were banned, and people who did not go to church or who tried to prevent their children from being sent to mission schools were punished, sometimes by imprisonment.

Over the last thirty years, the situation has started to change. Some Catholic and Episcopalian missionaries have begun to be more tolerant of Native American religion. A few now even regularly take part in such rituals as the sweat lodge.

At the same time, however, smaller Christian churches, such as the Pentecostalists and the Seventh Day Adventists, have become more active on reserves and reservations. Their missionaries often take the old-fashioned Christian view that native religion is devil-worship and that people who believe in it will go to Hell. In places where their influence is strong, these new missionaries often have a very destructive effect, dividing families and communities and weakening traditional culture.

TELEVISION

Even the most isolated Native American communities now have television. Many people feel that it has replaced the school system as the worst threat facing their cultures today.

Most Native American communities are too small and poor to have their own television stations. Because the programs they receive are mostly American or Canadian, they teach children to speak English rather than their own

◄ *Sweat lodge frames at Bear Butte, a Lakota holy place in South Dakota. Sweat lodges are used by traditional Native Americans for prayer and purification. Although Christian missionaries have tried to destroy Native American religion, thousands of young people are returning to traditional beliefs.*

▲ *A home on the Navajo reservation in Utah. Native Americans on reservations sometimes have to live in substandard housing with no running water or electricity.*

languages and to see the world through different eyes. One Oglala leader remembers: "When I was a kid, I used to watch Westerns on TV, and I was so brainwashed I'd be cheering for the Cavalry rather than for the Indians."

Through television, children are shown a way of life very different from their own and taught to think of it as normal. They are encouraged to want things that often are inappropriate to their own cultures and that they and their families cannot afford.

THE WELFARE CULTURE

As Native Americans have been forced to settle on small reserves and reservations, it has become impossible for most of them to live by traditional activities such as hunting. With no other way of making a living, many of them have become dependent on government welfare. There are some families in which welfare has been the only source of income for four generations.

The dependence on welfare has had a terrible effect. It is one of the main causes of the social problems in most tribes: the high levels of violence, suicide, family breakdown, and alcoholism. People who cannot work to support themselves and their families often lose their pride and their self-respect. They feel powerless to control their own lives and give up hope of ever being successful or respected by other people. Many of them feel trapped in a cycle of poverty and despair, and turn to alcohol or drugs as their only escape.

8 Images

Many Native Americans believe the worst problem they face is the images that other people have of them.

Ever since the first contact, other people have tried to fit Native Americans into their own view of the world. The first mistake was made by Columbus himself, who did not realize he had reached a separate continent. Instead, he believed that he had landed in the East Indies, so he called the people he found living there "los Indios."

THE NOBLE SAVAGE

To many of the first European explorers and traders, Native Americans appeared to be living in paradise. Unlike the countries of Europe, their societies seemed almost free of poverty, violence, and disease. People lived peacefully together, with enough food for everyone, and strangers were welcomed. "So peaceable are these people," wrote Columbus, "that I swear… there is not a better nation on earth."

"Are they human?"

Some early explorers believed that Native Americans were not really human beings. They thought they were just intelligent animals without souls, and that they could be killed like wild beasts. As a result, hundreds of thousands of Native Americans were massacred in North, Central, and South America.

In 1512, Pope Julius II, head of the Roman Catholic religion to which most Europeans belonged, finally decided that Native Americans were human and should be respected. However, many settlers continued to believe that Native Americans were animals and could be destroyed. Even in the twentieth century, Native Americans have been hunted and shot for sport.

Impressions like these soon led to the idea that Native Americans were noble savages, wild people who lived in harmony with nature and with each other and who did not have to work.

◀ *Although European settlers viewed Native Americans as noble, they couldn't understand their harmonious values or peaceful way of life. Because of this lack of understanding of the Native American life-style, Europeans called them savages. As with any group of people, stereotypes do not accurately describe anyone and are a form of racism.*

Many nineteenth century artists showed Native Americans as savages, which made it easier to justify taking their land. In fact, as this 1873 cartoon shows, it was often the settlers who were most brutal. It was the Europeans who first introduced scalping; a $10.00 bounty was paid for each scalp. ▶

Some Europeans despised Native Americans for being "uncivilized," but others envied their simple and natural way of life.

THE BLOODTHIRSTY SAVAGE

As soon as large numbers of settlers arrived and Native Americans started to fight to keep their land, many Europeans began to look at them in a different way. Now, instead of "noble savages" they were seen as "bloodthirsty savages" who killed and tortured innocent women and children.

Sometimes, Native Americans did massacre settler communities, although usually only after they had been attacked themselves. Much more often, however, it was the settlers who massacred the Native Americans. Many settlers did not consider Native Americans to be human beings like themselves who were trying to protect their country and their families. Instead, they felt that Native Americans were little better than wild animals, and that the only way to deal with them was to kill them.

▲ *A poster for a Wild West Show in 1913. Shows like this were very popular and gave people the idea that all Native Americans were fierce warriors who rode horses and wore feather war bonnets.*

THE WILD WEST SHOW

About a hundred years ago, an American showman named Buffalo Bill Cody created the famous Wild West Show. The show was similar to a circus, with hundreds of colorfully-dressed "cowboys" and "Indians" on horseback pretending to fight each other.

Many of the "Indians" in the Wild West Show were Lakota people, like the famous chief Sitting Bull, who had played an important role in the Plains Wars. By agreeing to appear with Buffalo Bill Cody, these Lakota actors were able to leave the reservations, where they were kept like prisoners and where they often did not have enough food for themselves and their families.

Cody took his show all over Europe and America. Through photographs and early films,

its image of Native Americans became familiar to people around the world. Millions of people thought that all Native Americans must be like Cody's Lakota riders: tall, silent warriors with horses, guns, and feather headdresses.

THE HOLLYWOOD INDIAN

Hollywood is the capital of the American film industry. Over the years, it has produced hundreds of popular Westerns that have been seen all over the world.

Many Westerns show Native Americans fighting American settlers and soldiers. Only a very few films try to give an accurate picture of Native Americans or explain why they were fighting. In most of the older films, the main Native American characters are played by white actors and speak in English rather than, for example, Sioux.

Most Hollywood Westerns have strengthened the bloodthirsty savage image of Native Americans. They are seen attacking settlers, kidnapping children, and torturing prisoners. A few films have presented the noble savage image instead. In *Dances With Wolves*, for example, the Lakota are shown as natural peoples who are being destroyed by the spread of European civilization.

Because these Hollywood images are so strong, many people still expect Native Americans to look the same as they do in films. Sometimes, visitors to a reservation will stop a Native American in modern clothes and ask, "Where are the Indians?" Since Americans have become more concerned about the environment, some have gone to Native American communities looking for a natural way of life. They have been disappointed to find that most Native Americans today live in houses and watch television.

Many Native Americans feel that the images of the past prevent non-Native Americans from recognizing the serious problems they face today. As Suzann Shown Harjo, a Creek/Southern Cheyenne political leader, says: "The problem is, people always think about us in the past tense."

◀ *A Navajo woman and child. Although Native Americans are rarely able to live as their peoples did 150 years ago, many non-Native Americans still think of them as continuing to exist in the old way, because of the stereotypes they see in films and literature.*

9 Native American resistance

Over the last 500 years, Native Americans have used many different means to try to defend themselves, their land, and their cultures.

WARFARE

In the past, many Native Americans fought heroically against settlers and soldiers. Tribes such as the Lakota and the Cheyenne in the Plains region, the Seminoles in Florida, and the Nez Perce in the Northwest held out for months or years even when they were hungry, poorly armed, and heavily outnumbered. Warriors such as the Oglalas Red Cloud and Crazy Horse and the Nez Perce Chief Joseph were great leaders, who won the respect not only of their own people but of the soldiers fighting them.

POLITICAL ORGANIZATIONS

In 1944, Native Americans in the United States founded the National Congress of American Indians to work politically for their rights. Since then, several other political organizations have been formed, including the American Indian Movement (AIM). AIM has organized many protests and demonstrations to draw attention to the problems in Native American communities. In 1972, for example, they organized a march called The Trail of Broken Treaties. Thousands of Native Americans from all over the country marched on the Bureau of Indian Affairs offices in Washington.

In Canada, Native Americans are represented by the Assembly of First Nations, as well as strong groups who represent regions and the separate nations.

Tecumseh

One of the greatest Native American military leaders was the Shawnee chief Tecumseh. At the start of the nineteenth century, he realized that Native Americans would lose all their remaining land if they did not stop settlers moving farther west. He tried to unite all the surviving tribes in a great alliance against the invaders.

At first he was very successful. Members of 32 different tribes joined him, and for a time he was supported by the British. He was killed in battle in 1813 while covering a British retreat.

LEGAL BATTLES

Many groups in both Canada and the United States have fought long court battles to protect their rights. Some of them have been very successful. For example, the Passamaquoddy and Penobscot tribes in Maine won back 30,000 acres of their land and $27.5 million.

◀ The Black Hills of South Dakota are sacred to the Sioux.

▼ A young Innu girl in tears as she watches her mother being taken to prison for trying to stop flights from the Goose Bay Air Base. The low-level flights from the base scare away the animals the Innu hunt and frighten people: although it is on the Innu's traditional land they have never been asked if they want the base to be there.

For other peoples, the struggle continues. The Oglalas and the other Sioux tribes are still trying to regain the Black Hills of South Dakota more than 100 years after the government stole the area from them. In 1980, the Sioux were offered $105 million compensation, but they refused to take it, saying the Black Hills are sacred and not for sale.

CAMPAIGNS

Groups throughout Canada and the United States are trying to stop damaging development on their land by publicizing their problems and asking for support from people in North America and Europe.

For example, traditional Navajos are campaigning to prevent expansion of a coal mine at Forest Lake in Arizona. The mine is owned by the British company Hanson, and in 1990 a group of Navajos traveled to London to complain about the project. They explained that, as well as causing pollution and health problems, the mine would destroy some of their sacred sites and weaken their self-sufficient sheep-herding economy.

In Quebec, the Grand Council of the Cree has been trying stop work on the James Bay project for a hydroelectric power plant, which threatens to flood their land. Recently, as a result of their campaign, the New York Power Authority dropped plans to buy electricity from the company building the dam, Hydro-Quebec.

The Innu, Canada, and NATO

During the 1980s, the Innu people learned that Canada wanted to build a huge NATO (North Atlantic Treaty Organization) Air Force base at Goose Bay in Labrador. The Innu realized that this would mean even more military flights over their land and would make their traditional life impossible.

A group of Innu women started a protest movement to campaign against the project. On several occasions, they entered the Canadian Air Force base at Goose Bay and set up camps on the runway to stop aircraft from landing and taking off. Hundreds of them were arrested and imprisoned.

In 1990, NATO announced that the new base would not be built. The Innu continue to campaign for the end of all military flights over their territory and for recognition of their land rights.

EDUCATION

Since the 1970s, tribes in the United States have been able to take over the running of schools on their reservations and set up their own colleges.

Many groups are using this new power to try to undo some of the damage to their cultures caused by the education system. In some schools, children now learn about their own language,

▲ *Cree children learning traditional skills by making snowshoes in school.*

history, and traditions, as well as subjects such as English and math.

The schools also offer courses in traditional culture, with tribal elders passing on their knowledge to younger people, while at the same time teaching skills such as computing.

In big cities like Minneapolis, where thousands of Native Americans now live, there are special schools where children are taught traditional values and beliefs.

CULTURAL RENEWAL

For most of the last century, the Canadian and U.S. governments have been trying to destroy Native American culture, but they have not succeeded in stamping it out. Traditional Native Americans in many tribes have suffered hardship, imprisonment, and even death to keep their beliefs and practices alive. In some communities, they have performed rituals and

The Wounded Knee Siege

In February 1973, Oglalas and members of the radical American Indian Movement took over the village of Wounded Knee (site of a massacre in 1890) on the Pine Ridge reservation. They set up a traditional tribal government and demanded that the United States recognize the Sioux's rights under the Fort Laramie Treaty of 1868.

The protestors were surrounded by more than three hundred armed police and troops. Two protestors were killed, but they managed to hold out for 71 days. Although the government did not agree to everything they asked for, the siege did draw attention to the problems of Native Americans and led to changes on Pine Ridge.

41

ceremonies in secret to keep missionaries and government officials from finding out about them.

Over the last thirty years, thousands of Native Americans have been returning to these traditions. Many of them are young people whose parents moved away from the reserves and reservations in the 1950s and 1960s. Growing up in large cities, they have realized they are not like other Americans and Canadians and want to discover their roots.

Probably the biggest change is the upsurge in traditional religion. Many people recognize that their identity as Native Americans is based on the spiritual relationship they have with the Earth. Traditional spiritual leaders have worked hard to preserve and pass on their cultures and have brought thousands of young people back to traditional beliefs and ceremonies.

10 The future

What is the future for Native Americans? After 500 years of destruction, will their culture be able to survive into the next century and beyond?

THE RETURN OF THE VANISHING RACE

Many Europeans and Americans have always seen Native Americans as a vanishing race who would inevitably disappear as European civilization advanced. A hundred years ago, that is exactly what seemed to be happening. The Native American population had fallen to less than 400,000, and some people predicted that Native Americans would have died out completely by the end of the twentieth century.

Instead, both in Canada and the United States, the Native American population has started to grow again. Today, there are almost ten times as many as there were in 1890, and despite their health problems they are continuing to increase at a faster rate than most other groups in North America.

▲   Dancers at the Oglala Nation Powwow. Powwows are held every summer in many parts of North America. They strenghen Native American culture and bring together peoples who have been divided by the reserves or reservations.

KEEPING THE LAND

The kind of future that Native Americans have will depend partly on the attitude of other people. If Native American communities are to be secure and successful, Americans and Canadians have to accept their right to live differently.

This means that the governments of both countries have to recognize rights to land, water, and resources. Groups who still follow a traditional way of life must be allowed to retain their territory. Other tribes need help to support themselves on their reduced amount of land.

▲ *Part of the Taos reservation in New Mexico. If Native Americans are to survive they must be able to keep their remaining land and resources.*

Because Native Americans are a tiny minority and have very little political influence, they often need help from other people in the struggle for their rights. There are several North American and European organizations that support Native Americans' campaigns. (For addresses, see page 47.)

THE RIGHT TO BE DIFFERENT

Native Americans want the right to be different, but they do not want to remain in the past. "People seem to think we're only Native Americans if we look the way we did two hundred years ago," one Cherokee said. "But you don't look the way your ancestors looked two hundred years ago. That doesn't make you any less European or American. And just because we wear blue jeans, we're not any less Cherokee."

Many Native Americans believe that they can use modern technology to strengthen their own culture. On Pine Ridge, for example, some of the schools use computers to make traditional Oglala beadwork designs.

Robert Grey Eagle, vice-president of the Oglalas' Community College, says, "We need to preserve the best of the past, and at the same time accept the best of the non-Indian world."

THE IMPORTANCE OF SURVIVAL

Many Native Americans think that it is important for their cultures to survive not only for themselves but for all people. They believe that Europeans and Americans are in danger of destroying the world and everything that lives on it through economic development and pollution. They feel that people everywhere need to learn from Native American attitudes and beliefs about the environment in order to save the Earth.

Charlotte Black Elk, a traditional Oglala who lives on Pine Ridge, explains, "When we pray, we don't pray for only ourselves. When we fill the pipe, the two-legged, the four-legged, the growing and moving things, the winged are all present there, and we pray for them because they are people too and they want to live. And so we view our struggle to maintain our religion, to keep the Black Hills, as not just for ourselves but so that everything in creation can live and live well. That all the people may live well together. That the Earth herself can live."

Native American Prophecies

Many Native American groups have prophecies about what will happen in the future. Some of them seem to warn of a disaster if people do not stop destroying the Earth and the animals and plants that live on her.

For example, there is an Oglala legend called The Prophecy of the Stone Child. It says: "112 years after humans cause the bear to leave the Black Hills there will come a time of great changes, a time called the Day of Blowing Skies." Some Oglalas believe this story warns of a nuclear war or an environmental disaster.

"So far as we know, there hasn't been a bear in the Black Hills since the 1880s," says one Oglala today. "That doesn't give us long to return the bear to them."

Glossary

AIM The American Indian Movement, a radical organization fighting for Native American rights in the United States.

BIA The Bureau of Indian Affairs, the United States government department that deals with Native Americans.

Bush Any area of land away from villages and towns where Native American peoples in Canada and Alaska go to hunt and trap.

Colonization Going to a country and taking land from the people already living there so that you can live on it yourself.

Hydroelectric power Electricity generated by water. It often involves damming rivers and flooding large areas of land.

Inuit People (sometimes called Eskimos) who live in the arctic areas of Canada and Alaska. They arrived in North America later than other Native Americans (probably about 4,000 years ago).

National Congress of American Indians The largest organization representing Native Americans in the United States.

Origin legend A story told by a tribe or nation to explain how it came into existence.

Potlatch A ceremony held by the peoples of the northwest coast. Traditionally, a chief or other important person would hold a great feast at which there would be singing and dancing and everyone in the community would be given presents.

Powwow A gathering where Native Americans wear brilliant traditional costumes, sing, and perform dances. Powwows, usually lasting a few days, are held in many parts of North America in the summer.

Pueblos Traditional Native American villages in the Southwestern United States. The houses are made of adobe bricks and they are usually built on steep hills. The Pueblo tribes live in these villages.

Racism Believing that other people are not as good as one's own people or treating others badly because they are of another race.

Reservation An area of land retained by a Native American community, or set aside for them by the government, in the United States.

Reserve An area of land retained by a Native American community, or set aside for them by the government, in Canada.

Shaman Someone who makes contact with the spirit world. Traditionally, he helped to find game animals and cured people who were sick.

Stereotype To attribute a characteristic to a whole group of people; the description is so general that cannot be accurate. Stereotyping is a form of racism.

Sweat lodge A small hut in which water and stones that have been heated in a fire are used to make steam. Traditional Native Americans use them for prayer and to purify themselves.

Tepee A tall conical tent, normally made from bison skin, traditionally used by the Plains tribes.

Totem pole A large wooden carving, sometimes using a whole tree, that is made by the Native Americans of the Northwest coast. Traditionally, the pole stood in front of a house and gave a kind of history of the family living there.

Treaty An agreement made between a two peoples. Often, the Native American nation gave up most of its land in exchange for the promise of protection and economic help.

Wigwam A house made out of wood and bark, traditionally used by Native Americans in the eastern U.S. and southeastern Canada.

Further reading

Bealer, Alex. *Only the Names Remain: The Cherokees and the Trail of Tears.* New York: Little, Brown and Co., 1972.

Callaway, Colin G. *Indians of the Northeast.* New York: Facts on File, 1991.

Flint, David. *Prairies and Their People.* People and Places. New York: Thomson Learning, 1994.

Henry Tall Bull and Weist, Tom. *Cheyenne Warriors.* Billings, MT: Council for Indian Education, 1976.

Hull, Robert. *Native North American Stories.* Tales From Around the World. New York: Thomson Learning, 1993.

Iverson, Peter. *The Navajos.* New York: Chelsea House, 1990.

Jones, Jayne C. *The American Indian in America, Volumes I and II.* Minneapolis: Lerner Publications, 1973.

Younkin, Paula. *Indians of the Arctic and Subarctic.* New York: Facts on File, 1991.

Further information

American Civil Liberties Union
P.O. Box 3012
Billings, MT 59103

American Indian Heritage Foundation
6051 Arlington Boulevard
Falls Church, VA 22044

Bureau of Indian Affairs
1951 Constitution Avenue NW
Washington, DC 20245

Minority Rights Group
379 Brixton Road
London SW9 7DE
England

National Congress of American Indians
804 D Street NE
Washington, DC 20002

National Indian School Boards Association
6001 N. Marble NE, Suite 4
Albuqueque, NM 87108

Office of Public Instruction
State of Montana
State Capitol
Helena, MT 59620

Survival International
310 Edgware Road
London W2 1DY
England

Index   Numbers in **bold** refer to pictures as well as text.